There and Here

There and Here

Maureen Korp

First Edition

Hidden Brook Press
www.HiddenBrookPress.com
writers@HiddenBrookPress.com
EST. 1994

Copyright © 2021 Hidden Brook Press
Copyright © 2021 Maureen Korp

All rights revert to the author. All rights for book, layout and design remain with Hidden Brook Press. No part of this book may be reproduced except by a reviewer who may quote brief passages in a review. The use of any part of this publication reproduced, transmitted in any form or by any means, electronic, mechanical, photocopied, recorded or otherwise stored in a retrieval system without prior permission in writing from the publisher or a licence from The Canadian Copyright Licensing Agency (Access Copyright). For an Access Copyright licence, visit: www.accesscopyright.ca or call toll free: 1.800-893-5777.

There and Here
by Maureen Korp

Art by Damon Kowarsky
    Cover: rooftops mont saint-michel, 2017
    Page x: B-57 Canberra, 2011
    Page 71: aermacchi mb, 2009
    Page 97: cairo interior II, 2003

Cover Design: Richard M. Grove
Layout and Design: Richard M. Grove
Author photo page 101: Sylvia Klein, Ottawa, 2020

Typeset in Garamond
Printed and bound in Canada
Distributed in USA by Ingram,
       in Canada by Hidden Brook Distribution

Library and Archives Canada Cataloguing in Publication

Title: There and here / Maureen Korp.
Names: Korp, Maureen, author.
Description: Poems.
Identifiers: Canadiana 20210328487 | ISBN 9781989786543 (softcover)
Classification: LCC PS8621.O7865 T54 2021 | DDC C811/.6—dc23

one's not half two. It's two are halves of one

e e cummings, 1944

Contents

Part I: The Aviator Cinquains

    1.0 Pre-flight Checks – *2*
    2.0 Lift-Off – *16*
    3.0 Off Radar – *30*
    4.0 Pilot Error – *44*
    5.0 There and Here – *58*

Part II: Heresies

    OAHU – *74*
    i.e.d. – *75*
    Another Explosion – *76*
    11.11.11. – *77*
    Remembering – *78*
    The Garden – *79*
    Friday Afternoon – *80*
    Checkpoint: Khyber Pass – *81*
    another saint's tomb – *82*
    Tienamen Square, Beijing, June 1989 – *83*
    5 July 2013: Four Copts killed outside Luxor,
            in Dab'iya Village, Egypt – *84*
    Marsyas – *86*
    today, tomorrow – *88*
    Heresies – *89*
    Brookford Road, Syracuse – *90*
    Winter Ice – *91*
    Camera Obscura – *92*
    Chalkidiki– *93*
    Arizona Cactus – *94*
    the sake cup – *95*
    Poem for Henry Dumas (1934-1968) – *96*

Earlier Publications – *99*
Acknowledgements – *100*
About the Author – *101*

Part I

The Aviator Cinquains

*dedicated to Tim, Bill, Hamid, and EMK,
my father*

1.0 Pre-Flight Checks

1.1   the flight
formation: geese
ducks, F-14s, 18s —
same principle: twinned, slipstream—one
out front

1.2	sun to
dark formation
what matters is where you
are inside the wing and changing
places

1.3   the flight
            leader turns the
            wing, the one out front, all
            the rest . . . all the same, shift, turning
            in place

1.4   I did
               not know any
               of this out on the field
               watching birds, airplanes, all heading
               somewhere

1.5	so I
	waved because I
	believed the pilot could
	tell grandma he'd seen me here in
	Texas

1.6   Ft. Bliss,
            imagine . . . a
            place with a name like that,
            Ft. Bliss, Texas—knife-sharp heat, snakes
            insects

1.7 being
dirt poor was just
temporary hard luck,
and assigned quarters near the
airfield

1.8 out there
in the desert
quiet, quiet . . . at night
horses and wagons, travellers
quiet

1.9   I could
       see them from the
       window by my bed and
       no one said where they were going
       either

1.10	she was
always singing
all the time, my mama
about wishing she were single
again

1.11   red hole
             clearly marked . . . ping.
             brown-red matted fur, and limp
             jack-rabbit claws. dead beast bigger
             than me

1.12	bullet
wound, daddy said.
"Let's fly, girl." straight up, he
threw me . . . high in the sky, so high
I cried

2.0 Lift-Off

2.1	midnight
and no telling
where we're going—all the
same and all right, love, just to be
going

2.2 you told
me you loved me
sleeping here in your arms
when I awakened . . . should I have
spoken?

2.3   we see
ourselves centered
on our own horizon
line. that's true. come stand here in front
of me

2.4

you make
me believe in
Daedelus, Icarus
each flying free, each calling, "look
at me . . ."

2.5 watched you
bite into an
apple, the human heart
has rhythmic openings . . . chambers
come here

2.6   the heart's
cavities are
two, symmetrical . . . and,
the brain has four, paired like the heart
right, left

2.7   early
      in the morning
      your voice . . . leaving, ground fog . . .
      cold, heading off . . . new route, flight time
      maybe

2.8   under
           the wing, empty
           air . . vacuum, that's what keeps
           propeller planes up . . . as for jets?
           that's faith

2.9   see me
         alongside you —
         everywhere the birds fly
         flight formation, fluid lines, fine
         spirals

2.10   ducks, geese
        mate for life, you
        said . . . but, what if one dies
        first, then what happens in the flight
        pattern . . .

2.11 they change.
mid-flight, wing shift
repositioning . . . it's
a throttle hold: heartbeat, breathe in
breathe out

2.12   coming
        up outside, full
        throttle, smoothly giving
        way to another coasting back
        slipstream

3.0 Off Radar

3.1   wing struts
                schematizing
                all the world above, and
                below . . . everything flat out for
                distance

3.2   air to
        air lightning and
        everything moving in
        and along . . . between the cloud, star
        and moon

3.3 grid lines
up, down, across
navigation schemes laid
upon planes—earth, sea, sky . . . defined
visions

3.4 clear on
out, a new moon . . .
whiplash crescent, curving
perfectly above the clouds, and
the sea

3.5 straight line
of clouds breaking
east, ripping through morning
light.   contrails . . . cross purposes
misted

3.6 flying
in low, right, left
straight on clear . . . and that fast,
count the seconds slow . . . hard, red dirt
ahead

3.7 burning
fuel fast, twice
normal, soon reaching hard
tolerance—scorpion tails
whipping

3.8   it's that
            fast . . . turn the plane
            right-side up, no hope turned
            over . . . every eject means an
            injury

3.9   crash and
                burn, off radar
                nothing left, shards of clay
                kill holes, remains in boxes with
                numbers

3.10 nothing
else, but. . . thinking,
entry / exit . . . punched through
metal, glass, clay. no one found, no
one . . . him

3.11 gentle
as a fool, I
sit on the floor beside
the bed, knees drawn up to my chin
can't sleep

3.12   can you
        cut an hour
        like an apple, can you
        cut a life like a heart . . . I want
        to know

4.0 Pilot Error

4.1 there is
 a protocol
 for this sort of thing, a
 checklist . . . it puts everything back
 in place

4.2 combat
loops, atlatls
all flight patterns are long
throws, qualifying distances
thunders

4.3 the board
of inquiry
convenes in a room to
fix the blame; mere simplicity . . .
free fall

4.4   they went
off radar, no
one said more . . . not less, no
one took the blame, they are gone, don't
know where

4.5   when the
                sky broke open
                igneous rock marked where
                Icarus fell. . . Daedalus saw
                it all

4.6   as far
     as I could see
     the sky lay there . . . out of
     reach. . . how dare they, knowing that, not
     come back

4.7   he said
        any mistake
        kills, aviators don't
        get preferred odds. . . eagles do, not
        flyboys

4.8   did they
                know what tore them
                limb from limb, did they hear
                the crows shrieking when the sky tore
                open

4.9	I have
his letter with
me, can you see how much
he loved me, and I loved nightfall. . .
damn them

4.10   I'm fine
        they're missing . . . not
        dead . . . please, no pain killer
        this pain is mine, it's all I have. . .
        not now

4.11   I want
to eat olives
by moonlight, and have a
place to come and go from . . . I want
him there

4.12   there, with
          reaching hands
          great, wide grin... and that hair—
          wild, everywhere his rich laugh
          tumbling

5.0 There and Here

5.1	before
	the deserts, sea
	waters, before the birds...
	land vertebrates knocked out... extinct
	not here

5.2   nothing
      out there, but stars. . .
      early morning echoes
      in the desert, and the silver
      first light

5.3   by the
       side of an old
       back country road, I found
       a rabbit's skull, picked white, clean . . . dry
       complete

5.4 thin, light
bone, delicate . . .
jackrabbits are superb
prey—smart, like coyotes, no raw
gut fear

5.5   there and
here, we are where
we need to be, so they
say. . . I do not know what is meant
by that

5.6 quiet,
frail as a
glider—sometimes men die
in bed, all wood splints and linen
memories

5.7   cloudburst...
        thunders, when it
        comes, hear them drumming on
        the world's rim, all the dead, before
        and now

5.8   matches
       and cigarettes,
       all my mother ever
       wanted . . . day and night I ran to
       get them

5.9 the light
is beautiful
through the trees. . . soft evenings,
leaves scattering. . . someone's come home
next door

5.10 out there
in the desert
thirst, cold . . .people die
coming from somewhere, coyotes—
not them

5.11   some days
             the dust blows so
             fine, the sky becomes an
             overturned red clay bowl, fired in
             the sun

5.12   having
        hope is like that...
        a bowl of common clay,
        something made of nothing, hard to
        throw out

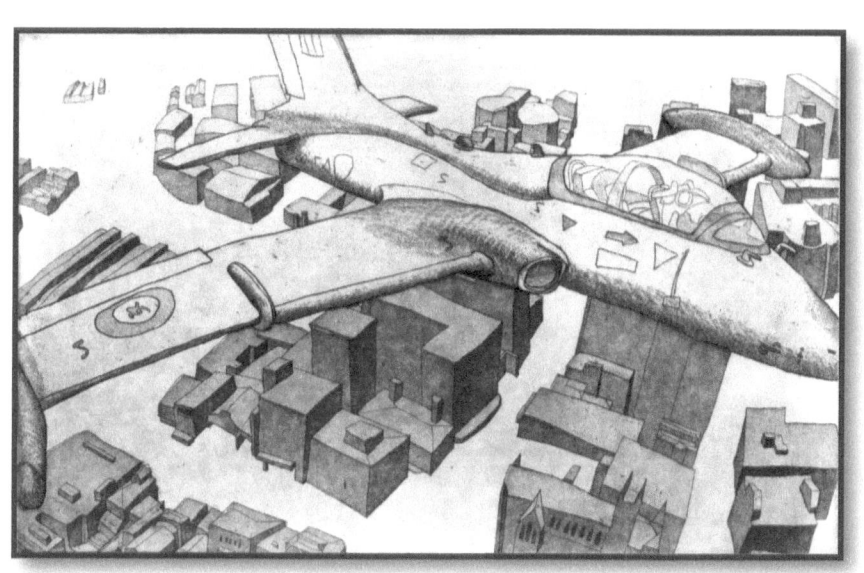

Part II

Heresies

dedicated to all those trying to get from one place to another

OAHU

seeing something there
a glint, quick light rippling
in the tide
half a heartbeat closer
dark, silvered triggerfish
back and forth . . .
back and forth

ships and planes and submarines
reconnaissance, surveillance—coastal
helicopters, back and forth, back and
forth . . .
in the tide, the triggerfish

in the boxes up the hill
all the numbers
all the bones, all that they could find
thrown upon the beaches
by the tides
back and forth, back and . . .
forth . . . nothing ever ends

i.e.d.

  improvised   never done this
    explosive   hold
          offside
          i.e.d.
    Who's walking point?
      Six dead . . . . do we tell?
          i.d.. . . . . i.d.   NOW
                  cover!!

Scr. . e. . e. e. e. . .ching harpies down in hell

Another Explosion

outside . . . dark
somewhere else
barricades, checkpoints
another explosion
when is . . . enough
enough
please
  I want . . . to know
  what . . . am I doing
here
pacing
one, one . . . one to the other
right, left . . . back again,
one, one . . . one to the other
outside
the barricades
when is . . . enough
enough

I heard you. I get it.   It's ok.
. . . don't look out
   turn out the lights
   you're here now. It's ok.

11. 11. 11.

a win,
a loss, who knows
any difference, in
the end, it's all the same. forward.
stop. here.

we're done,
no more
backwards, forwards, snake dance
advance into cratered fault lines
we're done

rows of
men, soldiers then
tired men, now
one by one,
all the same

each and every one of them
still unsure why . . . they are
here today
      move along
      one by one
we're done

Remembering

wave, cool on my shoulder
wave, cool at my back
inhale, exhale, inhale . . .
soft, love,
soft . . .
inhale, exhale,
tide going out
wave gliding
plucking the drift of sleep,
carry me into the sea
inhale, exhale, inhale . . .
bring me there again . . .
swimmer, sea . . .
        why did we go inland
     what reason was there
       to go inland
     so far from the sea

The Garden

Flowers are floating off
the trees nearby, their
slender branches
curving
into the last light of day

Quiet. Nothing more
is needed
we can stay here
another hour safely
before dark

Friday afternoon

camera crews here, there
tracking telephoto lens
sirens, noises, cries

raucous, crackling shrieks
somatic witness, skin stripped
raw. All gone wrong

gunmen in the mosque
men with bandoliers, and prayers . . .
bullets. here. young men

with guns, laden with
grenades. Soon the bodies stink
on rugs laid out for

prayer. The arguments
of faith, dismembered reason
flayed, drained dry, giddy

in the summer's heat.
blackbirds, crows wheel about
who will pray for what

Checkpoint: Khyber Pass

on a stone wall
gekkos, quick, clever
muricated insects,
barbed legs fastened hard
along the wall

over there
another dying beast
from the last invasion
a lioness, stay clear,
she's not dead yet

watch them all,
this, too
ends when legs fall off,
don't know when
nightfall

bury the dead
quickly, more than earth
is disturbed when it's turned
too often. move
get out. now

another saint's tomb

someplace else day starts
again, not here.   we stand
dry-mouthed, scared, bullets

clattering nearby
skin and bone already air
hands slipping free

of any creed or
place to be

all lost hope tonight
they've emptied the tomb
the body's disappeared

someplace else, daybreak
reason to pray.   not here . . . here
is hell. See for yourself

Tienamen Square, Beijing
June 1989

I saw his face that morning
live from Tienamen Square
one face
his fist
filled the television screen

"Take. Care. You."
"Take. Care. You. Self."

one voice punching
through lens, tape, satellite

13 hours difference inbetween
here, there
all the world away

his voice, face, fist, warning someone
behind the lens

"Take. Care. You."
"Take. Care. You. Self."

If I could, if I could do that . . .

. . . where are you . . . ? What
happened next?
No word since.

5 July 2013: Four Copts killed outside Luxor, in Dab'iya Village, Egypt

We lay them
one by one
heads wrapped round, swaddled under the chin
closing mouth keeps it closed,
in death, you see
jaws drop open
in death
air pushes out of the lungs,
sometimes we hear them shouting
sometimes they gurgle, too
we close their mouths, then no one will hear
another sound from the dead

The eyes of the dead are always closed,
yet they're not ever sleeping
they die with open eyes
every one of them trying to see what's coming next
we close their eyes when they die,
no one wants to know what the dead are seeing

That's just how it is.

Those men are fastening four into place
onto boards, holding them flat,
putting them into the ground,
white-shrouded Copts, poor souls
each with a paperback book on their breast
the covers are icons of Jesus reborn, like Osiris before
O writer, make something of this.

Marsyas

What a lad, what a song . . .
he played that flute
bird-song bright, quick-fingered notes
rippling up and down the spine
of every dancer's spin,
no one could outplay him, no one . . .
bet your life on that,
what a lad . . .
> *beat the drum*
> *stamp the feet*
> *no one can outplay him*

but maybe . . . a god   could . . . would . . .

Apollo shows up, with lyre in hand
> *let's play, kid*

Apollo is clever, grant him that, plays well enough,
holds that lyre . . .
>   upside-down, right-side up, pulls the
>   strings sideways, too. What a lyre . . . in his hand.

Everyone cheered, cheered loud . . .

Who played best? Marsyas? Apollo?
You want to deny the god?
                Deny Apollo?
We knew who played best.

See that tree . . . over there? That's where
they hung the boy, shrieking . . .
skinned alive,
hung the skin

      even higher, from that tree, that one
      over there

      Horrible, yes. What can you do?
The gods win every time, simple practicality—
Them. us. That's the difference.
                when gods play with men,
                  you're lucky to get out alive.

today, tomorrow

to be alive and
breathing . . .
        all it takes is air
        in, out
breathing . . .
just air . . . breathe
        in, out
        done
be here tomorrow

Heresies

If night were all day long
if moonrise and nightfall meant
never a change of day

if the late light of day
were never seen
in green-leafed alleyways

if all that were so,
and never once anything else,
then I could understand
daybreak,
prayer . . . .
and calls for death

Brookford Road, Syracuse

two deer
single file
crossing the road
in front of me
no sidelong glance, they know their way
I don't.
I can wait.

Winter Ice

faded blue shirts on white sheets
that's how I remember you best . . . .
your shirts washed clean,
       folded on Saturday

this morning, I moved over to
the other side of the bed,
       yes, still missing you

snow, this morning
hides last night's ice
insidious, persistent,
not much more to see . . .

beyond the vapours of
a noisy car idling,
going nowhere safely
today

Camera Obscura
for Michael

A simple box with one fixed lens
to focus light on paper,
light-sensitive paper
there, in the box.
That's the picture.
Give it time,
memory is sharp-edged
counterbalanced with regret.
Time unfolds in grey.
        Remember.

Chalkidiki

homesickness was something
I grew up with
homesick, even when I did not know
where I came from
homesick, for that place
where someone knew me,
even an empty grave with my name . . .
just might do

Arizona Cactus

In the desert, saguaro stand
big-armed,
      hard along the road.
Half are dead,
    half will be
in fifty years. Don't cry.
      Keep moving.
No one cries in the desert.
  Dehydration kills. Keep moving.
    The dead stand still. Keep moving.
        Remember me.

the sake cup

        one moment
I can hold for
        a long time
            in my hand, quietly
thank you, my friend,
      our fingers meet again

Poem for Henry Dumas
1934 – 1968

When he told me
in 1963, I was bleeding
told me I might catch blood
in my hands
and make poems,
I was only 18 . . .
sure didn't know his meaning,
all that drunk, black night
I just held on tight

The poet Henry Dumas, a black man, was killed by a white New York City transit cop at the 135th Street subway station in 1968. Reasons unknown to this day.

Some of the poems in this collection have been previously published. Thank you to all my editors for their trust in my writing. Those poems are as follows:

2 – "1.0 Pre-flight Checks" in *Soundings*. Christopher Levenson & Brian Camerson, eds. Ottawa: Buschek Books, 2005.

74 – "OAHU" in *nkarc*, 2:4, July-August 2018; and *vallum contemporary poetry*, 14:1, 2017.

76 – "Another explosion" in *VerseAfire,* June 2020.

78 – "Remembering," in *Glebe Report*, May 15, 2020.

79 – "The Garden" in *Lummox 8*, R.D. Armstrong, ed. San Pedro, California: Lummox Press, 2019; and *Anti-Terror and Peace*, Ada Aharoni, ed. Israel: International Forum for Litrature and the Culture of Peace, 2016.

80 – "Friday afternoon" in *TAMARACKS: Canadian Poetry for the 21st Century*. James Deahl, ed. San Pedro, California: Lummox Press, 2018; and *Anti-Terror and Peace*, Ada Aharoni, ed. Israel: International Forum for Literature and the Culture of Peace, 2016.

82 – "another saint's tomb" in *Lummox 7*, R.D. Armstrong, ed. San Pedro, California: Lummox Press, 2018.

83 – "Tienamen Square, Beijing. June 1989" in *nkarc*, 3:3, May-June 2019.

84 – "5 July 2013: Four Copts killed outside Luxor, in Dab'iya Village, Egypt" in *Window Fishing*. John B. Lee, ed. Toronto: Hidden Brook Press, 2014.

89 – "Heresies" in *Anti-Terror and Peace*, Ada Aharoni, ed. Israel: International Forum for Literature and the Culture of Peace, 2016.

90 – "Brookford Road, Syracuse," *www.Bywords.ca,* June 2019.

93 – "Chalkidiki" [formerly untitled] in *Ultra Best Short Verse 2016*, George Swede, ed. Toronto: Beret Days Press, 2016.

94 – "Arizona Cactus" in *Lummox 8*, R.D. Armstrong, ed. San Pedro, California: Lummox Press, 2019; and *Arborealis: A Canadian Anthology of Poetry*, John B. Lee, ed. Toronto: Beret Days Press, 2018.

95 – "the sake cup" in *VerseAfire,* June 2019.

96 – "Poem for Henry Dumas, 1934-1968" in *The Celebration of Poetry*, I.B. Iskov, ed. Toronto: Beret Days Press, 2021; and, *Canadian Forum*, Aug-Sept. 1984.

Acknowledgements

A number of writers have encouraged this work. Among them: Hanifa Alizada, Bill Bhaneja, Ronnie R. Brown, Henry Dumas, L. Anne Flammang, Avrum Malus, Blaine Marchand, Ana Olos, Brita Ostrom, Bernd-Uwe Schinzel, Ahsan Nadeem Sheikh, and William Sloane.

Not all are still living today; but, here it is, the book all were sure I would write about the worlds we know or knew once.

Thank you for your trust.

About the author

Maureen Korp is a military brat, the daughter of an American soldier. She grew up in faraway places, including Okinawa, Hokkaido, Oklahoma, Texas, Germany. She has also lived and worked in New York City, New Jersey, Pakistan, Ontario, and Romania. Home base today is Ottawa. She is an independent scholar, writer, art critic.

www.ingramcontent.com/pod-product-compliance
Lightning Source LLC
Chambersburg PA
CBHW021448070526
44577CB00002B/314